NATURE'S GIANTS

OSTRICHES

BY MARISSA KIRKMAN

WWW.APEXEDITIONS.COM

Apex is distributed by North Star Editions:
sales@northstareditions.com | 888-417-0195

Produced for Apex by Red Line Editorial.

Photographs ©: Shutterstock Images, cover, 1, 4–5, 6, 8–9, 10–11, 13, 16–17, 22–23, 24, 25, 26; iStockphoto, 7, 12, 14, 15, 18–19, 20–21, 29; blickwinkel/McPhoto/BFR/Alamy, 27

Library of Congress Control Number: 2023924595

ISBN
978-1-63738-940-9 (hardcover)
978-1-63738-980-5 (paperback)
979-8-89250-074-6 (ebook pdf)
979-8-89250-038-8 (hosted ebook)

Printed in the United States of America
Mankato, MN
082024

NOTE TO PARENTS AND EDUCATORS

Apex books are designed to build literacy skills in striving readers. Exciting, high-interest content attracts and holds readers' attention. The text is carefully leveled to allow students to achieve success quickly. Additional features, such as bolded glossary words for difficult terms, help build comprehension.

TABLE OF CONTENTS

CHAPTER 1

SWIFT KICK

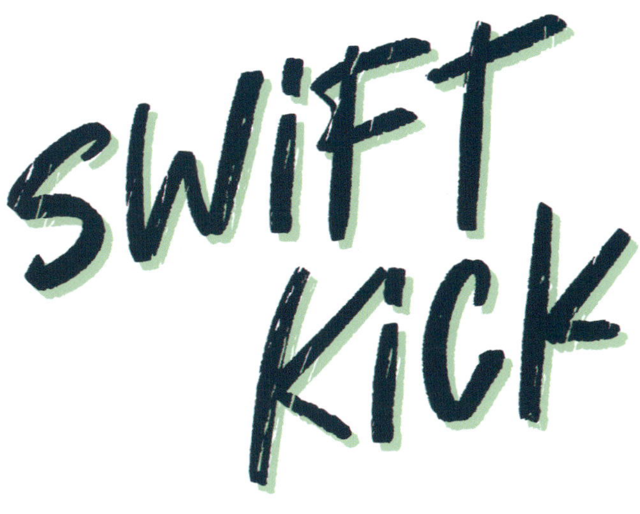

A male ostrich watches for **predators**. Female ostriches graze on grass nearby. Suddenly, the male makes a roaring sound. He has spotted a lion.

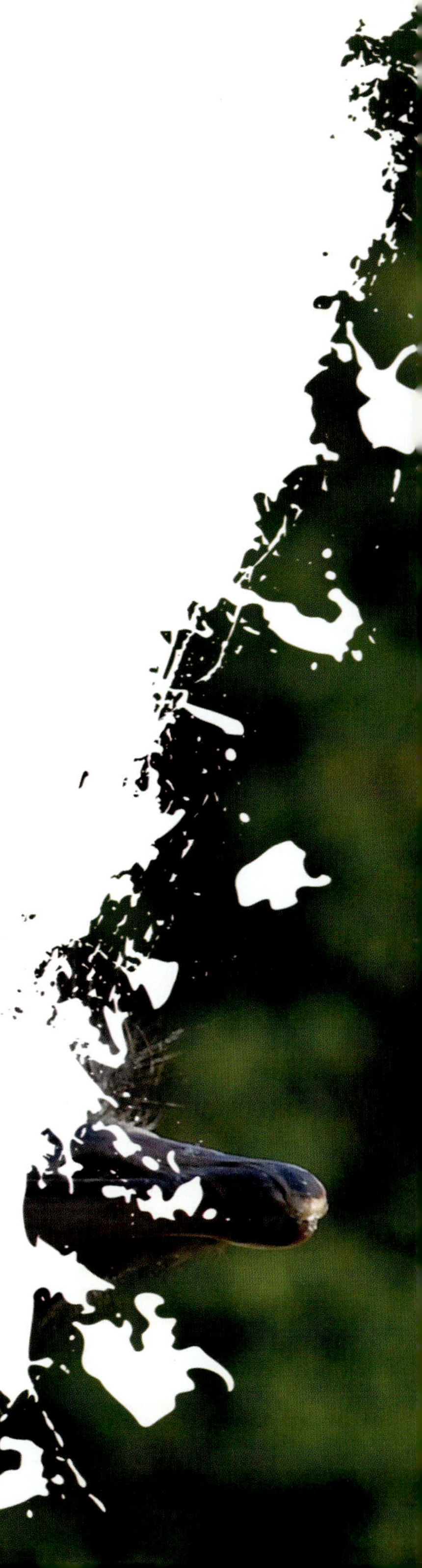

Male ostriches roar to warn other ostriches. Ostriches can also chirp, hiss, and honk.

Ostriches are the fastest two-legged land animal.

The lion runs toward the ostriches. The birds sprint away quickly. But the lion chases after the male.

FLIGHTLESS BIRDS

Ostriches can't fly. But they run up to 43 miles per hour (69 km/h). They use their large wings for balance while running. They stretch their wings out to quickly change direction.

An ostrich's wings can stretch 6.6 feet (2 m) wide.

The lion tries to bite the ostrich. So, the ostrich kicks with his powerful leg. His foot hits the lion's head. The lion is stunned. The ostriches safely run away.

FAST FACT

Lions, cheetahs, and leopards hunt ostriches. Vultures eat their eggs.

CHAPTER 2

BIG BIRDS

Ostriches are the largest and heaviest birds. They grow up to 9 feet (2.7 m) tall. They weigh about 345 pounds (156 kg).

Male ostriches are bigger than females. Males also have darker feathers.

Ostriches sometimes lie flat on the ground to hide from predators. Their necks blend in with the dirt.

Ostriches have long necks. Shaggy feathers cover their bodies. Females have mostly brown feathers. Males have black feathers with white tails.

An ostrich's eye is 2 inches (5 cm) wide.

GREAT EYESIGHT

Ostriches have bigger eyes than any other bird. In fact, their eyes are larger than their brains. Strong eyesight and long necks help ostriches look out for predators.

Ostriches have long legs. Each foot has two toes. The toes help ostriches grip the ground and run.

Ostrich claws can grow 4 inches (10 cm) long.

Ostrich legs are very strong. They help ostriches run long distances.

FAST FACT
Ostriches can cover 16 feet (5 m) in a single **stride**.

CHAPTER 3

DESERT DIET

There are two types of ostriches. Both live in Africa. Most ostriches live in **savannas** and grasslands. They can also survive in **deserts**.

Ostriches often live in dry areas with few trees.

Ostriches spend up to eight hours a day looking for food.

Ostriches mostly eat plants. They also consume insects, snakes, and lizards. Ostriches typically eat up to 4 pounds (1.8 kg) of food each day.

DESERT BIRDS

If ostriches can't find food, they can sometimes go two or three days without eating. Ostriches can survive for two weeks without drinking water. They get most of their water from food.

Ostriches have three stomachs. One stomach holds small rocks. The birds swallow these rocks. The rocks grind up the food. Other stomachs help **digest** the food.

Ostriches can eat plants that are too tough for most other animals to digest.

CHAPTER 4

Ostriches live in groups called herds. A **dominant** male and female lead each group. The other group members are females.

An ostrich herd can include 10 to 100 birds.

Ostriches lay the largest eggs of any bird. Each egg weighs about 3 pounds (1.4 kg).

The dominant male and female **mate**. Other females may mate with the male, too. Each female lays 7 to 10 eggs at a time. Ostriches sit on the eggs to keep them warm.

SHARED NEST

Females in a herd often lay their eggs in one nest. This nest may hold up to 50 eggs. The dominant female's eggs go in the center. They have the best chance of hatching.

Dominant male and female ostriches typically take turns sitting on the eggs.

Chicks hatch about six weeks later. Parents **protect** and care for them. After two or three years, the young ostriches are fully grown.

Ostrich chicks have soft, tan feathers with brown spots.

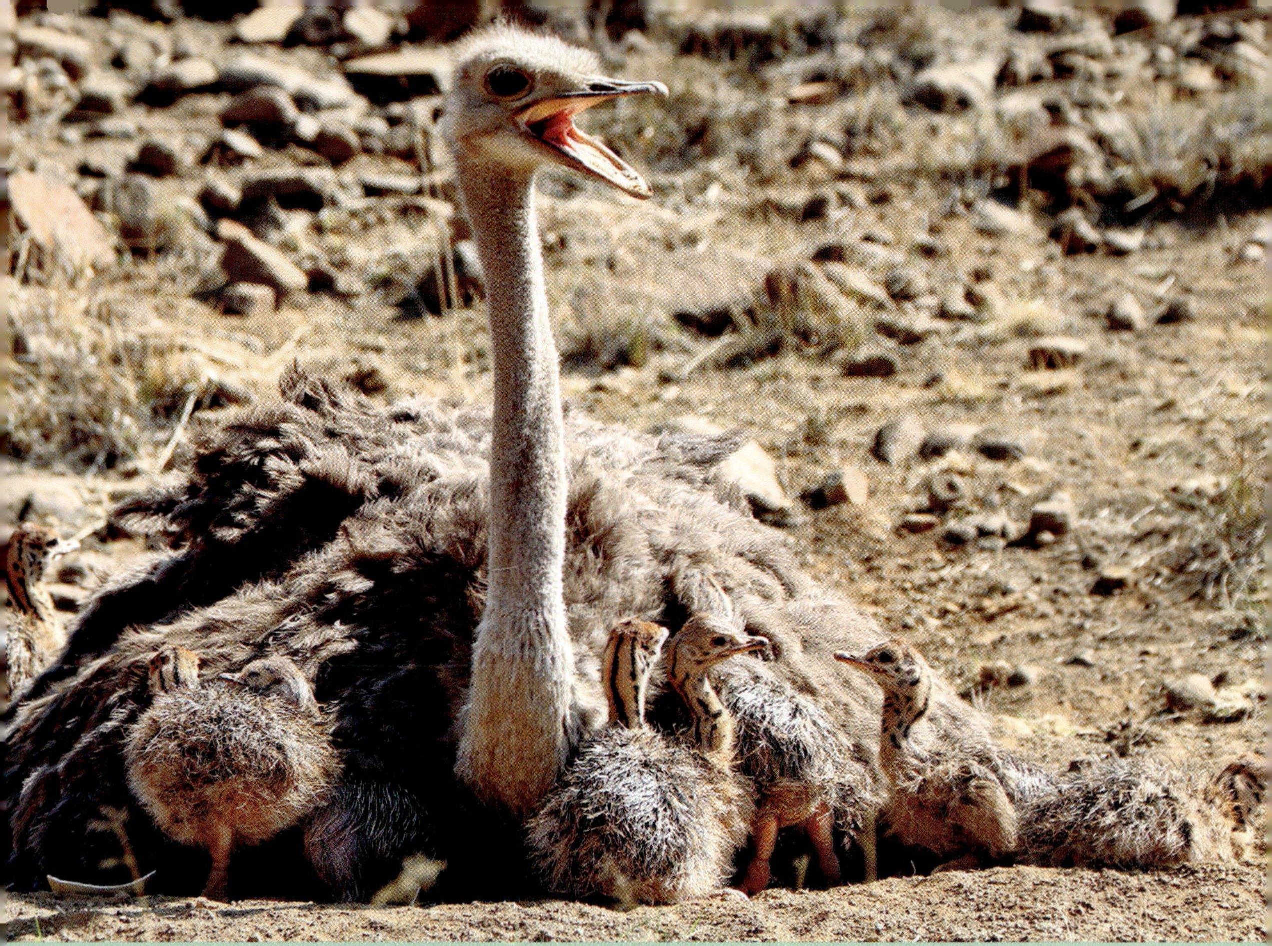

Ostriches cover chicks with their wings to keep the young birds safe.

FAST FACT

Ostriches can live for 30 to 40 years in the wild.

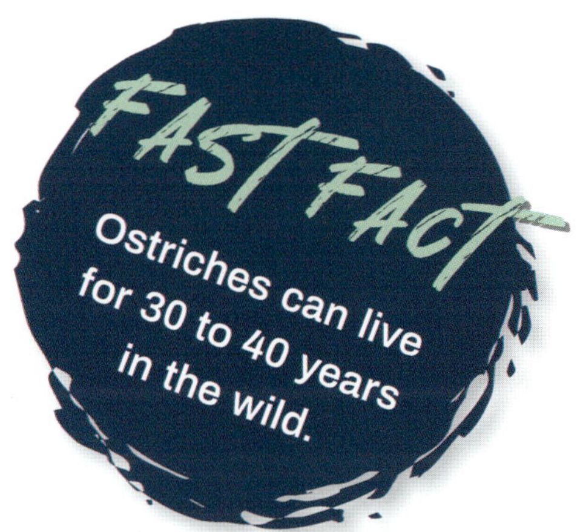

COMPREHENSION QUESTIONS

Write your answers on a separate piece of paper.

1. Write a few sentences describing what ostriches eat.
2. Which fact about ostriches did you find most interesting? Why?
3. How fast can ostriches run?
    - **A.** less than 16 miles per hour (26 km/h)
    - **B.** up to 43 miles per hour (69 km/h)
    - **C.** more than 50 miles per hour (80 km/h)
4. Why would getting water from food help ostriches survive in the desert?
    - **A.** Deserts don't have any food.
    - **B.** Deserts are dry and have little water.
    - **C.** Water in deserts is frozen.

5. What does **sprint** mean in this book?

The lion runs toward the ostriches. The birds ***sprint*** *away quickly.*

A. walk very slowly
B. hold very still
C. run very fast

6. What does **consume** mean in this book?

Ostriches mostly eat plants. They also ***consume*** *insects, snakes, and lizards.*

A. feed on
B. run from
C. roar at

Answer key on page 32.

GLOSSARY

deserts

Areas of land that have few plants and get very little rain.

digest

To break down food so the body can get energy from it.

dominant

The most important or most powerful animals in a group.

mate

To form a pair and come together to have babies.

predators

Animals that hunt and eat other animals.

protect

To watch over or keep safe.

savannas

Flat, grassy areas with few or no trees.

stride

One step, or the space that a step covers.

TO LEARN MORE

BOOKS

Humphrey, Natalie. *Ostrich: Colossal Bird*. Buffalo, NY: PowerKids Press, 2024.

Kirkman, Marissa. *Biggest Bodies*. Mendota Heights, MN: Apex Editions, 2024.

Riggs, Kate. *Ostriches*. Mankato, MN: Creative Education and Creative Paperbacks, 2023.

ONLINE RESOURCES

Visit **www.apexeditions.com** to find links and resources related to this title.

ABOUT THE AUTHOR

Marissa Kirkman is a writer and editor who lives in Illinois. She enjoys reading about animals, science, and history.

INDEX

ANSWER KEY:
1. Answers will vary; 2. Answers will vary; 3. B; 4. B; 5. C; 6. A